HEART AND MIND

Edited by

Heather Killingray

First published in Great Britain in 2003 by
POETRY NOW
Remus House,
Coltsfoot Drive,
Peterborough, PE2 9JX
Telephone (01733) 898101
Fax (01733) 313524

HB ISBN 0 75434 415 0
SB ISBN 0 75434 416 9

FOREWORD

Although we are a nation of poets we are accused of not reading poetry, or buying poetry books. After many years of listening to the incessant gripes of poetry publishers, I can only assume that the books they publish, in general, are books that most people do not want to read.

Poetry should not be obscure, introverted, and as cryptic as a crossword puzzle: it is the poet's duty to reach out and embrace the world.

The world owes the poet nothing and we should not be expected to dig and delve into a rambling discourse searching for some inner meaning.

The reason we write poetry (and almost all of us do) is because we want to communicate: an ideal; an idea; or a specific feeling.

Poetry is as essential in communication, as a letter; a radio; a telephone, and the main criterion for selecting the poems in this anthology is very simple: they communicate.

CONTENTS

III	Samuel Kindred	1
My Spirit Cries	Santal Bahh	2
The Old House	Wilma Nicholas	3
Desired Object	Rona Laycock	4
A Wing And A Prayer	Davide Bermingham	5
The Curtain Closes	Michael Alan Fenton	6
Children's Play	Heather Ann Breadnam	8
Stonehenge	Marion Whistle	9
Together	Rachel Abbey	10
Regrets - I've Had A Few	Christine Wylie	11
Fish-Dragons	Robin Adara Lewis	12
Prologue - The Cup And Saucer Tree	A R Lewis	13
Best Friends	Judith James	14
Stress Personified	Bobby	15
Virtual Love	Dalene West	16
When The Lights Go Out	Vicky Stevens	18
Kings Of Crows For The Day	Elizabeth Rait	19
Portrait	G Hunter Smith	20
Just In Case	T G Bloodworth	21
The Café In The Corner	Michelle Knight	22
Art Work	Ian Stephenson	23
A Tale Of Vanity	Jessica Ruggles	24
Truth, Or Not . . .	Marcus	25
My Hightower	Opal Innsbruk	26
Careless We Will	Natalie Sloper	27
A Winter's Dream	Farrell & Wright	28
This Changed World	Antonio Martorelli	29
Big Kids On Teenage Kids	Martin Henry	30
Patience, Patients	K Rowe	31
Snow Leopards	Derek J Pluck	32
Rain	Janet Robinson	33
Coming Home	Patrick McCrory	34
Shadow-Boxing	Mary A Shovlin	35
Time	M C Jenkins	36
In A Secret Sylvan World	Pamela Cox	37

Old Television	John Ball	38
Along Glitter Gulch	Paul Wilkins	39
The Bridge	Agnes Neeson	40
Seasons Of The Heart	R N Taber	41
Ms Knockout	Malcolm Peter Mansfield	42
Presumption	Muireen Dunn	43
Pantheism	Edna M Sarsfield	44
Waterfall	Pavandeep Kaur Mann	45
Masks	Judy Studd	46
Over The Ages	Lynne Walden	47
Rainbow	Elizabeth Hiddleston	48
Ode To A Sleepy Child	David Tiplady	49
One To Fifteen	Andy Botterill	50
Perseverance	Brenda Watson	52
How Lucky We Are	Gordon E Miles	53
Growing Up	William Rankin	54
Reminders	Diane Burrow	55
Marriage	Richard Wormald	56
Sabre, Lena, Lucy	Sue Colson	58
For Three Church Bells	R Wiltshire	59
Unconditional Love!	Wendy-Elezabeth Smith	60
Family Life	Viv Eckett	61
The Lost Generation	Phil Clayton	62
It's Your Life	Dan Russell	63
Entwined	Jean Gill	64
Anxious Heart	Iris Davey	65
Computer	Graeme Vine	66
The Jewels In His Crown	Pamela Carder	67
Ear To The Ground	Candice-Leigh Johnstone	68
Platelayers - My Friends	R L Harvey	69
Never Work With Children And Animals	Susan Seward	70
The Short Cut	Vann Scytere	72
Virus Direct	Hazel Sheppard	73
Please Excuse Me	Jane Milthorp	74
Knickers - I've Worn Them All	Adele C W Lane	75
Satisfaction	Diana Mudd	76
To Set Free	Eileen Barker	77

The Real Romeo And Juliette	Marisa Greenaway	78
The Loch Ness Monster	Margaret Meek	80
The Hoover	Alister H Thomson	81
If You Can . . .	Raymond Spiteri	82
Massive Mammories	Jackie Manning	83
Fun To Be Had . . .	Carol Moore	84
The Things You Girls Will Do For A Little Extra Cleavage!	Kim Swales	85
A Funny Poem	Irene Roberts	86
A Disputation	William Sherratt	87
Misnake	Paul Rand	88
Lads' Army . . . Revolting Rhyme	D Shiels	89
Sixty	Geoff Fenwick	90
The Barmaid's Farewell	Patrick Brady	91
Psychic Vampire	Kate Marsden	92
These Petite Three-Liners	Allan Bula	93
Sad, But Hilarious	J Lucas	94
Untitled	Frances Maguire	95
A Slave Or What?	Kathleen Townsley	96
I Had A Dream . . .	Karen S E Mason	97
Never Too Old	Maureen Williams	98
Laugh And Grow Fat	T Sexton	99
Absences	Norman Bissett	100
Life	Marie Barker	101
Danny	Stephen Mead	102
The Virtuous Pen	Ailsa McDermid	103
Thank You My Spirit Child	Meg Aku Sika Millar	104
Organised	Jerome Kiel	106
Peace	Joan Kingscott	107
Washday Blues	S Greenhalgh	108
Steam Iron . . . Sssssss	Aleene Hatchard	109
Acceptance	M J Hawkins	110
To Lorna	Ernest Staeps	111
Good Shot	Vann Scytere	112
A Poem Tells A Story	G Wilyman	113
A Ruby Rare	Derek J Morgan	114
Glossop's Heroes	Pam Cole	115

Starlight Express	T Lawrence	116
Live In Peace	Antoinette Christine Cox	118
Morning	Mary Cathleen Brown	119
Black Dog	René James Hérail	120
Goodbye My Son	Doreen Hughes	121
My Friend	Rachel Kate	122
Call From The Sky	Lozina Taylor	123
Haunts Of A Past	Michael McLellan	124
Forgive Me If I Cry	Stephen A Owen	126
Out There	George S Johnstone	127
The Dead Man's Chest	Paul McGranaghan	128
Immortality	William Pegg	129
From Love Beads To Space Seeds	Teresa Whaley	130
The Ascent Of Man	Michael Gardner	131
Casablanca	Carole A Cleverdon	132
Mirror In The Hall	Mary Morley	133
All Change	Joan Mathers	134
I've Got My Head Stuck In The Railings	D A Sheasby	135
Joyride	S R Thompson	136
Asunder	Jean Medcalf	137
Isolation	Judy Balchin	138
The Kitchen Clock	A M Drever	139
Angry Elements?	Norman Meadows	140

III

The irony, I suppose, is mine alone.

Some of me will stay in the dirty light
of the all-night shop,
where words turn to marbles in my throat
and I just reach out for you.

Other things I can't have.
Afterwards, for example; the four of us
sitting together on a night too cold for September,

or you,
seeming nearly bloodless on the crimson sofa.

Samuel Kindred

MY SPIRIT CRIES

My *spirit* cries like the sad wind -
biting and venting its anger on a millennial world;
which drags my battered memory,
to the desperate plight of the pigeon,
resorting to ravens begging prayer for food -
survival that my overworked conscience dreads
and flashes like a beacon,
warning an uncaring world -
of the dangers to come,
when pigeons or ravens of the wild,
would have to knock on empty doors for sustenance;
endangered species would have been extinct
but only just highlighted in a world
without reins as I've always lamented.

Have you ever wondered who feeds the birds?
Curiosity that has led me to haunted
territory without regret;
wildlife or creation as a whole,
we all need food for survival;
prayer is not enough but paves the way for action to follow.

Santal Bahh

THE OLD HOUSE

The old house long deserted, stands forlorn
Still holding secrets of our childhood years,
She never ceased to listen to the fears
Of those she cradled safe within when born,
Their faded pictures still her walls adorn.
There, darkness echoed sounds of silent tears
Into the night, the sobbing disappears
And hope once gone awaken on the morn.
In solitude alone two decades past
Bereft of love and laughter in the air,
Then in that world of silence came at last
The sounds and smells that rooted out despair.
That house, our home, was never an outcast
And never will we end our love affair.

Wilma Nicholas

DESIRED OBJECT

Faint dew on your skin
my fingers trail down your shallow cleft.
In the sunlight your skin gleams with a Nubian sheen
and your purple depths are like the night sky in winter.

Cool and smooth and dark,
what is hiding beneath the membrane?
You are the late harvested mystery, the darkly forbidden fruit.
I can smell your seductive perfume, rich and ripe on my hands.

Holding you so very gently
I raise your roundness to my face
pressing you into my mouth I tear your flesh tenderly
I feel your juice run past my tongue with almost
unendurable sweetness.

See the wound I made;
surprisingly yellow, the yellow of wild honey.
I watch curiously as your precious life's essence bleeds slowly
pale and thin anointing my hand, I am transfixed by its lustre.

I pierce your flesh again
solid, unyielding, unwilling to play my game.
Defiantly different, so now I cannot breach your defences.
What a trickster, what a Judas, you hid your callousness so well.

You have a heart of stone.

Rona Laycock

A WING AND A PRAYER

In days of old from cultures bold, men did dream to
reality, it would seem, of change to come, hoping to
light the night would run.
Sometimes perceived, yet not intentionally deceived,
to tell the talk and let all men walk with open heart
and carefree mind.
Truth will out, 'tis a great find.
Is the bird in flight on a wing and a prayer?
Is it not I who dreams of flight? But when awake
to whom I tell, I do not dare -
for I did choose long ago; my avian spirit to where I go.
Swift and sleek with down-curved beak, the fastest of all
they say, to dine on the weak.
High in the sky o'er land and sea, blue birds did fly
chased, and chased by me. They cried freedom,
my spirit the same and in the morn there was no blame.
Hanging in the air for all to see,
the man who dreamt his green land free,
to be allowed that dream was not seen fair
he'd come too far on a wing and a prayer.
Feathered and flighty my spirit did leave,
crying out to the people, do not grieve.
Your day will come, they'll accept your plight,
your spirit remains strong, it'll not take flight.
Now in the light, high in the air, I tell you all,
yes I do dare, you've come far and done well
on a wing and one million prayers.

Davide Bermingham

THE CURTAIN CLOSES
(Machina-ex-Deus = something not human)

The curtain closes
on the ignited chariot
incinerating the shell.

White smoke proclaims
the whim of life

leaving a wake of memory
logging the tears
of days remaining.

In time, death shall wipe
away those tears.

The ebb and flow of sound,
practised by the choir,
with clash of chords
played on rocks of disbelief.

The bass return from horizons afar
with soprano and tenor in unison,
their dimensions reflected
from stained glass windows.

Rope-pulled bells plead
humbling human dilemmas
and overweaned ambition
with upward thrust
of cathedral hope.

Pray for wisdom
for they shall hear
but only if they will listen.

Cleansed of race and religion
remembering the one entity
created the Earth for all
- in life and eternity.

Michael Alan Fenton

CHILDREN'S PLAY

I love to hear the children play,
They play in the road, and in the park.
It's not as often now though,
The computer takes the part
The art of play and friendship
Is disappearing fast.
Children just want the TV on.
Conversation is a lost art
So it is a large pleasure,
To hear the children play.
In summertime I lift the net
And show I am there.
But they really don't mind at all.
I don't interfere or correct them
    Right or wrong.
I love to play soft music.
It makes me feel so good.
Together, it brings back childhood memories
And it is so good.

Heather Ann Breadnam

STONEHENGE

Stark against the skyline
The stones stand, towering,
Out of the dawn, the rosy dawn.
Listen, at first light, and discern
Echoes of primeval voices, chanting, chanting;
Aeons away, and yet
As yesterday.

Proud, unmoved by history
And its passing pageant-parade;
Mute, but with a meaning beyond words
The stones stand:
Question without an answer,
Theorem hewn from the substance of man's mind
But with no solution,
Until the Earth's last sunset
When the final shadows are cast.

And even then
The stones will just crumble, crumble and fall,
The last and truest timepiece of them all.

Marion Whistle

TOGETHER

The day we met I was in
Mourning
The time we met I refused
To see

I lived with my memories
Nothing more
Despite a future brighter
Than ever before

After three months of rejection
Three months of 'just friends'
The guilt and regret at last seeped away
As you taught me how to walk away

Now three months
We
Have been stubbornly
Waiting

For our time to dawn
When we shall meet again
And the past is buried
Not shunned

As we finally move on together
And face the future . . . as one.

Rachel Abbey

REGRETS - I'VE HAD A FEW

I worked to get my A-levels three, no teenage larks and romps for me,
No midnight hikes along the downs or boys to cause a father's frowns.
I worked through University - a first or nothing it must be!
No mad rag stunts or term-end balls, no midnight sneaking into halls.

I chose as husband one who was an embryonic finance boss;
We wined and dined, new clothes I wore, 'til surfeiting became a bore.
My envious friends drifted away. I couldn't pass the time of day
With them or meet for tea unless it benefited me.

I worked so we could buy a sound system with the noise all round
Which let you hear the cellist sigh. I did not hear my children cry.
I did not see my son's first step through business-lunching with a rep
Or notice when my daughter lost three stones at catastrophic cost.

At her bedside, with time to muse on what I had to gain or lose,
I vowed that earning life was done and four could live on wage of one,
Discovered value in an hour which did not bring me any power
Or monetary gain. I found my husband I could still astound!

Now I'm alone, and what's to show for half a century of 'go'?
My daughter's gone to find Shangri-La with a youth in a
                              Reliant Robin car,
My son is modelling underpants for a dubious firm somewhere
                              in France,
The husband who scorned 'weak' woman so has a pseudo-blonde
                              bimbo forever in tow.

And I have the time to watch flowers grow, and talk to stray cats,
                              and say more than 'hello'
To my son and daughter when - sometimes - they ring, and watch
                              television, write stories and sing,
And marvel at rainbows, and bake my own smells, get muddy
                              in meadows bejewelled with bells
And watch the late films then stay sleeping 'til ten - make up for
                              the teen years I missed out on then!

Christine Wylie

FISH-DRAGONS

High up on the roof ridge
we dream of home
beneath the eastern sea.
Ochre scales and fish tails,
we sit and stare,
great jaws gaping,
yawning with boredom
at our silent lot:
to spout a timely rain
in every threat of fire.
This is the way of it:
all must earn their keep.
And what else can we do
but charm away the lightning
and never pause to sleep?

Robin Adara Lewis

PROLOGUE - THE CUP AND SAUCER TREE

Insects humming to green sun-speckled leaves,
Rays of bright sunshine dancing with flitting shadows,
All tuned to the touch of the summer breeze.
That's how it was and has always been.
And will remain. Secured in my mind.

As a young boy I gazed up at your beauty,
Admiring the curve of your saucer shape.
I stretched, jumping to view your cup,
Longing to climb you to taste your splendour,
Knowing that now we were bonded together.

When at last I climbed into your world,
I knew I was safe, nothing could harm me:
Your embrace, my own secret sanctuary.
Always when pain or danger threatened,
My mind would race to be safe in your cup.

Broken bones, hospital smells, schoolmasters' canes,
All failed to inflict any pain.
Hardship and danger, from Dunkirk to the Rhine,
All were as nothing and easy to bear:
You came to my aid, you never failed me.

When, as a boy, I lay down in your cup
To dream and plan my life-adventure -
I knew that you would always be there
To shelter and guide me wherever we went.
My haven - my harbour - in the tempest of life.

A R Lewis

Best Friends

This morning my best friend wouldn't speak to me.
I tried several times but was blocked,
Dismissed, excluded,
For no reason I could see.

Agitated, I could not think what to do
Without the one who shared my thoughts.
Supportive, constant.
I must get through.

Panic too - so much of myself has gone.
Our work - my letters, poems and dreams
Denied me in a flash.
I am quite undone.

Uncomprehending, I wonder - can I redress
Any unwitting harm to my valued friend?
Despondent, frustrated.
I must have access.

Desperate, I phone for help. A calm voice gives the key.
Rename C:\programs\windows\wpcset.bif to wpcset.lae
'WordPerfect for Windows' reappears.
Hallelujah!
My best friend speaks to me.

Judith James

STRESS PERSONIFIED

The stress inside
I cannot hide.
It's here to stay,
Personified.

The more I think and fight,
The more it'll hurt tonight.
So I'll choose silence
Over risking violence,
Against this parasite.

I'm not very sure
Why it didn't arise before -
Kept hidden for so long.
I must stay strong
Because now I can't ignore.

Bobby

VIRTUAL LOVE

Click
hello . . . a/s/l?
I read.
You said
you wanted to
meet me
in your room
and I looked in mine
and glanced at the mouse
inside my house
the lethal, silent, still and powerful mouse.
In your room,
where you sat and spoke to me,
I fell in love
and was helped by a mouse
in the house.
So silent was the screen
where I saw your words.
I fell in love
with your mind
and you, with mine
and, it felt fine
and the mouse
looked on
and helped us fall
and I felt tall
as
my words (and yours)
trailed a path of cheese
for the mouse
in the house
in our room
and trailed off
into the cold

when you wanted to meet
the cold got feet
and it was mine.
And the mouse
sat still
but our fingers not
as we shared a tot
of love in a glass.

Dalene West

WHEN THE LIGHTS GO OUT

Silent echoes ricochet from a
Situation he can so vividly recall,
The repulsion of war mirrored in his eyes.
He was an inexperienced draftee still
Holding onto his mother's apron strings,
When they put a rifle in his hands.

Now all he's left with are visions
Of blooded shrapnel and bullets
That filter out his views on reality.
His soul's been left not far from death,
His heart on the crimson front line.
He screams himself to sleep each night
Wishing that the end would come
When the lights go out.

Vicky Stevens

KING OF CROWS FOR THE DAY

Crows in a half-turfed field
A runway of brown against the green
One crow finds a tussock
And ascends it eagerly
'I'm the king of the castle!'
Squawks he.

Elizabeth Rait

PORTRAIT

A Cornish beauty, with style and grace.
Lovely beyond compare.
Longing for a lover lost?
Yet hope is hiding there.
Someone will come, but he will see
Only heartache as she sighs
Never knowing of the secret, behind her sad brown eyes.

G Hunter Smith

JUST IN CASE

My affairs are all in order,
The will's made out, it's true
But don't get optimistic,
There's nothing left for you!
Just simply getting older,
Brings several things to mind.
Remembering those who helped me,
Thank you for being kind!
I take the local paper,
Obituaries I read
Just making sure that I'm not there,
Right now, that's all I need!
Don't think I'm in a hurry
To go, of course I'm not
But dying is expensive,
The price is rather hot!
I passed the undertaker's
Window shopping, seemed ideal.
Just see your name engraved in stone,
I wonder how you'd feel!
No one knows for sure what time,
We might be 'called away',
My advice to one and all,
Live life, enjoy each day!
We all have little problems
But that's the human race.
I'd better get my skates on
Pack a bag though - just in case!

T G Bloodworth

THE CAFÉ IN THE CORNER

My second special place
was a little café right in
the corner of the old bull ring
in Birmingham.
Now sad to say it's
no longer there because
they are re-doing the bull ring.
It was a nice little café,
always very busy.
I used to go there a lot
with my mum when I was younger.
My mum was well-known and liked
in there by the owners.
I'll miss that little café in the corner,
I also miss my mum.
Going in the café in the corner,
it wasn't the same without my mum,
I never went in there after losing my mum
very much, too many memories.
I used to stand outside
and look in and I used
to picture my mum and me
sitting in there. She used to
have a cup of tea and I used to have
a glass of milk.
I think we managed to sit
at every table in there
but her favourite table
was the one in the middle
of the café in the corner.

Michelle Knight

ART WORK

A
Cormorant
Dips

Surfaces

Frisks head
Applausively.

Is it
A bird
Now?

- 'Black bottle
With fish' -

Says the label!

Ian Stephenson

A TALE OF VANITY

Beauty gazed out of the mirror,
The fairest of them all,
Peaches and cream, a rosebud mouth and golden shining curls.
Young men all stared and stuttered,
When she came into a room,
Her haughty air repelled them all,
She laughed them all to scorn.
Until one day her blue, blue eyes alighted on a soldier,
Whose uniform of scarlet made her hard heart shudder.
Alas her parents did not view
With elation this liaison -
Soldiers were low in their esteem,
As having no rich connections.
So off to Gretna did they run,
To tie the knot of marriage,
Hoping the parents would come round
And make them rich and happy.
This was not so and, truth to tell,
Poverty did not suit them,
Three children later - beauty gone,
Grey hairs among the golden,
No time to look in mirrors now,
No snobbish airs and graces,
Just work and want,
Watching her man lose money at the races!

Jessica Ruggles

TRUTH, OR NOT . . .

Reflections see what you try to hide,
unable to look back as he looks forward.
People see nothing but an outer swathe
but he sees an impugn abyss.
Watching, waiting to attack the weak
mind in your hour of need, not his.
Consuming your soul while you sleep,
devouring your psyche in mid-sentence.
Never knowing the strength at which
he'll feast on your sanity, leaving you
with nothing but an empty plate.
Nowhere to hide, the street, each shop
window reaches out through the
milling people as if there were mist
shaking you unreceptively to death.
Like a funeral pyre engulfing your
self-worth, even the ashes of the
person you once were.
And all that would be left, is an empty shell.
(Like others on the beach)
Till you are true to yourself and others.

Marcus

MY HIGHTOWER

Oh, woe was me!
What more could happen in my life
To bring me down - I thought
First the floods and then the fire
And theft - all conspired to make me homeless
Must pull up roots and move away
To another town no less
In order to obtain a place . . .
A rented council flat.
Oh - woe is me!

Settled in and by the grace
Of some charitable friends
The basic comforts of a home
Were mine - at last some rest.
Up and down the lifts I went
Running down the stairs whenever
The lifts did not move fast enough
For me.

Oh, this is fun - the flat is great
People everywhere!
Up and down the lifts they go
Chatting everywhere
Morning! Morning everyone
What a view from here
Oh, I am so glad that I
Moved away from there!

Opal Innsbruk

CARELESS WE WILL

Let my words fall down
And bury themselves in your heart
So they may become a part of you
Run with me and the wind
Let us tangle your hair
Through meadows of thick
Green summer haze
Let the hum of the clear
Night sky send you to sleep
While I dream next to you
Of things we could do
And what we have become
Let me and sunrise greet you
With 1,000 smiles of a new
Day, happiness
What carefree things
Shall we do today my dear?
Time stands still and thoughts
Become nothing more than
Time consuming thinking
One thing we will not do today
And another one million
Careless we will

Natalie Sloper

A WINTER'S DREAM

The firelight flickers
Defying the darkness that wraps this winter's day.
Through the frosty glass, all is still and quiet
Only the tireless shadows dance on.
I'm happy to just sit and stare into the fire's flames
Thinking of futures and dreaming of the past.

My face warms and I move back slightly
Sinking into my armchair.
I stare hazily at the silent evergreen
In all its decorated splendour,
And remember the happy Christmas nights
This old room has seen.

Gradually,
The crackling fire turns into the laughter of young children
And the dancing shadows turn into their games.
And there I am, a young man again
Contentedly watching my children at play,
And smiling at the young woman
Who shares those happy times with me.

Then the fire stirs in its torment, and reality spins me round.
I start to call to the children, but before I make a sound
I realise, that was then and this is now.
I was in another world,
A world I took for granted,
A world I thought would never end,
A world that is now merely a winter's dream.

Farrell & Wright

THIS CHANGED WORLD

I often think why so much has been changed in our world.
We have lost the way and the know-how to live a happy life
and be nice to our neighbours. But now we kill each other.
What happened to our society? Most people today
have no morals of good and perfect society.
I ask myself what is going on in our street today
with the present society? It is not very nice. There are too many killed.
Murder and assassination and too much violence
to the very young girls. What happened to the good neighbours
that once flourished in every street? In England and the rest
of the world. Nobody hears or sees anything.
I am happy that I am too old, because I do not like to live
anymore in this changed world.

Antonio Martorelli

BIG KIDS ON TEENAGE KIDS

I am one of the older *kids* - a second childhood
And when I see the kids today, my thoughts are far from good.
Their manners and their actions, my sad soul rarely heartens,
The shapely girls with mini skirts, long legs - and then Doc Martens.
The boys who with their baggy slacks and shirt tails hanging out
Are rough and inconsiderate; the essence of the lout.
The radios and mobile phones, the noise and scruffy bustle
They negotiate in strident tones and then resort to muscle.
Perhaps they are a touch more 'green' and care for the oppressed
But virtue tends to stay obscured among the badly dressed.
What hope is there for home and hearth with such a generation?
Where can we turn for comfort and the future of the nation?
The doctors, lawyers, scientists, the diplomats and others
The politicians, engineers and future caring mothers?
A thoughtless generation who are rushing to damnation
Will drive the 'old and wiser' to the brink of desperation.

But then I cast my mem'ry to the heyday of my youth
And, through a little mistiness, come face to face with truth.
The kids are sullen, brash and coarse, anathema to me
But then, in my first childhood, that's how *I* used to be.

Martin Henry

PATIENCE, PATIENTS

As you lay in your hospital bed
Thinking that you're nearly dead,
With things stuck in arms and chest
Wondering how you're going to rest.

Spare a thought for the nurses there
Looking after your every care,
Working right throughout the night
Making sure that you're alright.

And when a new day dawns
We wake up full of yawns,
They come in from the night before
And still they managed to do their chores.

Making beds and fetching pans
Even holding someone's hand,
Listening to all our moans
As if they had none of their own.

Each one looking fresh and bright
All in all a pretty sight,
Staff nurse marshalling up her troops
Putting students through the hoop.

And when time comes for you to go home
Aren't you glad you weren't alone,
Just think of all they've done
Angels in white, every one.

K Rowe

SNOW LEOPARDS
(Banham Zoo)

Yawning, at ease with the lowland forest of the zoo,
But sprung-alert by faint reflection or dim shadow
On the large glass panels that we view you through;
Still wild enough to care about making an easy kill,
Muscles ripple beneath the grey, thick-pile carpet
Of your fur, as your body's form appears to flow
Along the tree-trunks, placed strategically,
In a creative eerie twilight of the large enclosure
And the almost liquid green of your captivity;
Tail, almost as long as body, keeps your balance
And dense-furred, snow-shoe paws ensure
Sure-footed progress in the drama on this stage -
As the headlamps of your eyes stare into my soul,
Illuminating my experience and haunting conscience
With the conflict of your being here at all. Not for you
The high white silences of the Himalayas, bitter cold
And hunger your only and almost constant companions;
Here freedom compromised by comfort, well-fed
With no likelihood of death from poaching or starvation,
Your fur no coat to satisfy some human vanities
And body parts not contributing to folklore remedies -
You are the bright future of your endangered species,
A beacon of hope and burning need for conservation.

Derek J Pluck

RAIN

Sparkling lights - highlighting the dark sky.
Rain hitting the windows.
Wind howling, knocking against the trees
Leaves go flying, leaving a trail to walk through,
Cold, damp; a young girl runs quickly past
Clutching a paper over her head.

Janet Robinson

COMING HOME

Oh Ireland dear I love you so, your meadows o' so grand
I have been away for forty years, and now I am coming back
To now enjoy my Irish life on the land where I belong
I'll walk again those grand old lanes on heather hills of home
Each night before I went to sleep, I said my prayers to God
And told Him what I wanted most
To see my Irish home
America is so far away and full of Irish folk
But no matter who you talk to, it's always on your mind
Ireland, my home

But now my passage I have booked and coming home to stay
And when I do arrive, a cottage I will buy
The roof thatched with golden corn and white-washed all around
The sale is arranged to purchase and a new start I will make
I will modernise this cottage but also burn the peat
There's a garden back and front too and busy I will be

When I get this cottage back to life and furnished all anew
I will go and visit Katie who is a widow near to me
I'll look her up and tell her, although I'm second best
That I want to make her happy and know some happiness too

We should not ever have fallen out, but then we were so young
I joined the American Police Force but I never forgot you
So now that I am home again where we left off
I never did get married for I always thought of you
I spent these years all in the forces and sergeant I was made
But God has been so good to me that you are still around
And on you Katie I will spend some of these dollar bills

Patrick McCrory

SHADOW-BOXING

Deepest, darkest night
Witness angels' fight
Outside my window
Michael 'gainst Luc'fer
The proof it is there
You are in the know

Wait, is it a fact?
Do burglars attack?
I lie on settee . . .
The moon out of sight
Ravished in the night?
Or could it be
- Trees?

Mary A Shovlin

TIME

what we all possess
what use we use
what we own
in many ways
apart from work
and play
daily portions every day
hopes and dreams we plan
we strive to gain
progress the name of the game
rich, middle class and poor
all strive to profit
moment by moment
hour, hour by hour
week by week
month by month
time slips by very quickly
time is not our friend
not in any way, time
time is what we have to employ
allotted year by year
progress our purpose
it's done this way
every season has a reason
time passes away
then it's over, gone
life is spent we have no
more time

M C Jenkins

IN A SECRET SYLVAN WORLD

In a secret sylvan world
A little hour you spent with me
I cast a spell in aery magic
To bind you closer than a shadow.

In the silent sable of the night
When the restless leaves are still
And you are deep in peaceful slumber
Yet your spirit shall not sleep.

Though unseen still you shall feel me
Wrapped about you as a mantle
A sweet and gentle golden memory
Turn your head and know my touch.

If you should ever cease to love me
The leaves within my heart would die
And falling bring eternal winter
Spring could never come again.

Apart and separate yet not divided
Feel the frizzon down your spine.
Time will turn and in its turning
Another interlude will bring.

For the various loves of a man
Complete the man and his life.

Pamela Cox

OLD TELEVISION

in their boxes heard and
not seen colours
picturing magic from the sky
black and white merging into grey
a story in the signal
it is the unseen 60s
the agony of a mother
and only child crying in
the pouring rain
wet litter blowing
through the streets
as men fall out of pubs
electrical lightning strikes twice
a memory of years long gone
but it seems like yesterday
monochrome drama rained into
my room

John Ball

ALONG GLITTER GULCH

It's an area of Las Vegas
Where sunglasses are worn at night
To counter the frogspawn of neon
Dark ladies of the night
Sneakily sip bourbon with their burgers
As another jet lands at McCarran
Stretch limos cruise
Silent boulevards
And air conditioning
Breaks down
In baking motels

Paul Wilkins

THE BRIDGE

Quiet calmness, quiet happiness, quiet joy
Silent thoughts, silent words, silent feelings

All the stars around
The silence of the night
The darkness of the world
The bright moon, high above

The night speaks words never heard,
Thoughts never spoken,
Feelings never allowed to live,
But always the bright moon, high above

Music, a whole world to be explored
A world to relax in
A place to hide in when the world is crazy
A love the generations can share
Brought together many times by songs of the moon

Darkness engulfs us, surrounds us
The chilling night air settles around us
For some the time to sleep
For others the most amazing time
But always a moon guarding the sky

Always proud high in the sky
Building unseen bridges to countries
Reuniting families, long unseen
Rekindling dying loves
Flooding back long lost loves
Bridges to many cultures
Bridges to some families
Bridges to a few souls
Never closed, never jammed
Always there, always strong,
The *moon bridge.*

Agnes Neeson

SEASONS OF THE HEART

My love came with the swallow
that nests in spring;
in fairest flight I'd follow
and hear the bluebells ring

My love, it sang loud and clear
across earth and sky
for the whole world to hear
though some deny

For my love, it is gay
nor less fair for that;
and whatever they say,
truth will out

Come winter's freezing chill,
together still

R N Taber

MS KNOCKOUT
(Dedicated to Sharleen)

Initially he had seen her around
Her voice a sweet, welcome sound.

First she had hit him with her smile
That took him back awhile.
Then she simply followed through . . .
With a cool, upright: 'Hello',
Which brought him to attention
Left smarting from the you know
Embarrassing glow.

She finished him off
There and then
Like she did
With most men.

Using her by now famous
Lingering side glance . . .
Applied with such an air of confidence,
A real killer blow . . .
He didn't stand a chance.

Who could resist 'Ms Knockout' . . .
He was a conquest no doubt.

Malcolm Peter Mansfield

PRESUMPTION

As she drew together the curtains at her window
Trembling with every move she made then suddenly gasped
Breathless, silently afraid
She took gentle steps to get to the nearest chair
And almost jumped out of her skin
Hysterically she laughed
So loud, so very loud, saying, this is only my thoughts.

Muireen Dunn

PANTHEISM

Secure within its hallowed walls a godhead one in three,
no pomp or circumstance of sound unveil its mystery.

Nor would all knowledge imparted thus
that lays beyond the pale of man.
In darkness mirrored, a glancing truth
reveal its plan.

Not teeming spires and imagery
whose pantheon of fine array,
books historic, testaments our
hopes and fears allay.

A paradox of pantheism,
this enigmatic soul of man
the table's laid for thee!
Whoever sups will know in part
and glimpse eternity.

Edna M Sarsfield

WATERFALL

Ferociously pounding the ground
Like a torrent of tears.
Gurgling like a mass of babies
Spreading foam all around.
Marching down the mountain
Not caring to be quiet.
Gleaming in the sun
Yet shining in the moonlight.

Pavandeep Kaur Mann

MASKS

Searching for existence in the puzzle that is me
I try to find reality; a reason just to be
Do I wear a smile today; do I wear a frown?
Shall I scream and shout today or shall I be a clown?

Will I have some purpose to take me through the day
In this meaningless existence will I find my way?
I want to show my anger; I want to show my pain
Yet when I try to be myself, I'm knocked down once again

The maze of life's confusion leaves me right out on a limb
A search for true identity has made my vision dim
This crazy world we love to hate has left me standing still
There must be meaning somewhere this aching void to fill

I need to search for answers but where do I begin?
A creature of captivity securely bolted in
The people who are close to me say my soul is well
Is there a key to turn this lock; release me from my cell?

So; it's either on a soapbox or turn the other cheek
Would that make me strong as steel; would it make me weak?
Truth and confrontation might get me through the fight
But ships on alien courses float aimlessly through the night

There is one conflict left to choose - silence or speech
Both contained within my grasp yet simply out of reach
Silence shall be golden when the truth alone is told
I will discard my mask today; risk it and be bold

Judy Studd

OVER THE AGES

From Dark Ages to digital
Horse and carriage to Concorde
Our lives are forever changing
More than we can afford.

When we meet our friends
We would stop for a chat.
Now, with life in the fast lane
There is no time for that.

Powered things are everywhere
From a motor car to a toothbrush
But despite these mechanical aids
We seem always in a rush.

The countryside is covered in concrete
For industry and the need of a home.
Gone are the green fields and woods
Where as children we would roam.

This is all called progress
So we can live in a better place
Give us back the simple life
And the smile on a child's face.

Lynne Walden

RAINBOW

The rain falls from the sky, cascading over
The land, swelling rivers and streams,
Thunder booms and crashes,
Lightning flashes,
Nothing stirs in this miasma of sound.

The rain stops, blue sky shows on the far horizon,
Everywhere water drips, rustling the sodden leaves,
A slight breeze fans tree branches,
Small birds flutter their wings, they believe the storm
Has passed, in its wake a rainbow.

It stretches across the sky in an arc of light and colour,
The vivid hues vibrant and glowing,
Mauve, purple, orange, indigo, white,
The children point in wonder at this awesome sight,
'Oh Mummy, can we go in search of its end,' they chant.

At the end of the rainbow is the pot of gold,
This is the legend we are all told,
But one has never found the end of this phenomenon,
For it is a myth, a story good for the soul,
The rainbow, God's magic, a vision to behold.

Elizabeth Hiddleston

ODE TO A SLEEPY CHILD

Come along my child,
Let's get your pyjamas on,
It's time to get you ready for bed.
We've had a long day of fun and games,
It's time for you to rest your head.
Go to sleep my child,
Dream the sweetest dreams,
Of castles in the air,
And candy apple trees.
If that bogie man scares you,
And you wake with tears in your eyes,
I'll do my best to comfort you,
And wipe your tender cheeks dry.
So go to sleep my child,
It's time for beddy-byes.

David Tiplady

ONE TO FIFTEEN

'Ball in hand, keep the ball in hand,'
the coach screams from the touchline.
'If you kick it away again,
I'll bloody murder you
when we get back in the changing room.'

The players can hear his voice,
but can't hear it at the same time.
Too much is going on.
If he can do better,
he should be out here
putting his body on the line.

It's no use shouting.
They're a bigger and better team.
You can only tackle so long,
as their flanker picks up the ball
and has another run.
You can't keep stopping him.

Scrum-half to fly-half
to centre out to their wing.
Blood drips from a cut in my chin
as I await the next collision.

I dip my shoulder and try to put
another man down with weary arms,
only to end up in a heap
in the mud for my trouble,
but have made the tackle all the same,
stopping another score for the time being.

The rain beats down.
I'm soaked to the skin.
My fingers are numb.
It's a good half hour
since I could feel them.

I wonder why I do this,
Saturday afternoon after Saturday afternoon.
Is it meant to be fun?
No, it's the love of the game.
That's the only logical explanation,
for all of us, one to fifteen.

Andy Botterill

PERSEVERANCE

You've taken the plunge,
your feet have left the bottom
they're off the ground, splashing,
you're treading water,
it seems frightening.
Now there's a balance to be found,
strokes to be learned -
it isn't easy
(did you think it would be?)
but you're working very hard.

You knew you had to try,
yet feel you may not make it
you'll be overwhelmed, sinking,
limbs are aching,
it feels painful.
But then you find the balance,
you've got it right -
it wasn't easy
(did you think it would be?)
but you're swimming at last.

Brenda Watson

How Lucky We Are

How lucky we are who have a home,
When it's cold and wet, we are nice and warm,
We have food to eat and things to drink,
TV, radio and books to read that make us think.
People to talk with and games to play,
A nice warm bed to sleep the night away.

But those outside without a home, what do they have?
A shop doorway or under a bridge, their bed
A box or perhaps some coats for warmth.
I know that some prefer that way but others have no choice to stay
On the streets that are cold at night.
How good it would be if the homes that are free
Could be filled with those who are out in the cold.

Gordon E Miles

GROWING UP
(Dedicated to my granddaughter, Gillian)

From childhood into youth we grow
Unblemished yet by living
Impatient now to find and know
By curiosity driven.

To sample tastes of adult fare
Like drinking beer and smoking
That first fag lit with cocky air
Leaves us spluttering and choking

The secret puff, the furtive drink
Those things experimental
Should serve to make us stop and think
How much they're detrimental

And so we grow we test and try
Soon find out for ourselves
Those habits others may live by
Are best left on the shelf.

William Rankin

REMINDERS

They shout and laugh.
Something reminds me
of my mortality.

Dictate a time to celebrate,
fireworks, apportioned glee.
Something reminds me
of my mortality.

They try, proclaim a way
to say: live for today.
Something reminds me
of my mortality.

The drug forget, beget
another day,
dig for the future, set
along a groove, forget
responsibility
it's too dour.

Something reminds me
of my mortality.

Diane Burrow

MARRIAGE

The day resounded with it. I had seen
that morning as if it were played on a screen
the felling of a block of flats at New Cross.
For some weeks it had been apparent to us
who make the long trooping haul
up the line that its face was marked to fall;
the comfort of surrounding houses gone,
it stared with concrete eye blankly at the sun,
coldly and greyly it filled the air,
holding no anticipation, empty of despair.

Still we were surprised to feel a judder rip
up the lines carrying up to us the whip
of the discharge. It shook the carriage.
I thought of distrust breaking into a marriage
car. It was more than unexpected; surreal
to watch the tower twist and reel
and then in a compressed accelerating rush
fall. Our expectations were mixed into the crush
of its capitulation. No one quite knew
how to gauge the perspective of the collapsing view

But the electric morning sky seemed
to digest the shock of it and the air teemed
with a visceral blueness where the slabs had stood.
I thought of Mons, which we had visited,
of the flaring petrid quality of its light,
pervasive, thin, as if backwashed with white.
(There is a skyscape painted into limestone plaster
of the church there, which once defiant of disaster
still catches with prescient exactitude
the steepling, balancing, high value of altitude.)

The train jerked on, joggled past the moment.
Some people murmured, made remarks, intonements
uneasily weighing the heft of what had occurred.
But what? For collectively we demurred
from naming the loss, that a thing standing
could be so *elapsed*. That the noise of its landing
thrown out to those of us who chanced by
could be all that was left of it. It suggested why,
secretly, we all value that which we can grow to hate
procession, order, things regimented, the straight

vertical lines that we construct in the shallows
of the atmosphere, the breakwaters, the narrows
of orderliness set into the water. Structure
is not always strength. It can rupture
and break, and it can betray the emasculated
muscle beneath. Yet within us, encapsulated
by our frame is the need to raise high up,
make balance. How does marriage (tying up
our elemental senses) set them in concrete,
house us, harbour us, make us complete?

Richard Wormald

SABRE, LENA, LUCY

Three Labradors - all rescue dogs,
Sabre, Lena and Lucy.

Sabre - tall and lean,
Liked to carry things and barked a lot!

Lena - short and squat,
Jumped about and barked a lot!

Lucy - didn't carry things and hardly gave a woof,
But jumped around the most!

Three Labradors - no more,
Except within our hearts -
    And pictures on the wall . . .

Sue Colson

FOR THREE CHURCH BELLS

In the reign of Victoria, gentry farmers
and mill owners were at loggerheads over Corn Laws.
In the reign of Elizabeth II, Thatcher and conservationist
fight the straw wars;
A dispute over thatched cottage aesthetics,
'Long wheat straw bad, combed wheat-reed good' argue
conservation critics,
'Long straw looks shaggy, 'poured on' and is not suitable for replacing
The thatch originally of combed wheat-reed of a listed building.'
Time was when a country lad followed in steps of his father
But now anyone can attend a thatching course; sales rep
to deep-sea diver!
So it's work up for grabs, bit like a barn conversion
A matter really of cost effectiveness, not one of conservation.

R Wiltshire

UNCONDITIONAL LOVE!

She holds him with sheer delight,
squeezes and kisses him,
sleeps contented, wrapped in his arms,
he loves her, trails his fingers softly
through her long blonde hair,
laughing together, both unafraid,
whispering conspiratorially, they look
my way, I smile, jealous not,
no angry words from me, his wife,
no tears of sadness do I shed,
I silently watch them, trusting,
knowing nothing and no one can
harm her now,
her hand in his, they walk away,
suddenly he swings her high,
holds her, loves her, more than words
can ever express, she is 'flesh of flesh',
blood and soul, our granddaughter!
Sophie, our daughter's child.

Wendy-Elezabeth Smith

FAMILY LIFE

When will they give me peace and quiet, my mind cries out to me.
If it's not the telly blaring out, it's their crazy music pounding loudly.

Then their dad comes home from work, 'Oi! You two
Keep the noise down,' he shouts at the top of his voice!

Someone's knocking at the door.
The dogs start barking madly, the parrot squawking too.
'Anyone gonna answer that bloody door?' hubby yells out angrily!
Meaning me?

Oh! Just to sit and daydream or
To wander around the garden without the kids shouting,
'Mum, have you washed my football kit? What's for dinner,
You know I don't like fagots.'
'I can't find my maths book. He's calling me names again, Mum.'
'No, I'm not, if you grass on me again, I'll smash your face in.'

Then my hubby, bless his heart!
Turns to me and says, 'You look exhausted love, why don't you
Finish washing up those dirty dishes and make a nice cup of tea,
Then come and put your feet up.

Oh, by the way, before you do, there's something I've got to tell you,
We're overdrawn at the bank; our cheques are bouncing too.
But don't you worry love, you just come and put your feet up
And have a nice cuppa with me!'

Viv Eckett

THE LOST GENERATION
(Lest we forget)

At the going down of the sun,
Will we remember them?
Who? What? Where? When?
Those who gave their tomorrow
So we could have our today.
What sacrifices the lost generation made,
Where they lay in an unmarked grave.
A mother's precious bairn.
When another Hitler makes his mark again,
Do we shrug our shoulders -
Thinking it's not our problem?
As the sun rises,
Will we remember them?
Who? What? Where? When?

Phil Clayton

IT'S YOUR LIFE

Hammer down on the hammer line
Looking good and feeling fine
The lights are green so you may go
Cos it's your life and it's your show

Bury the past deep in the ground
The way is up, stop looking down
Your lights are on right at the start
Cos it's your love and it's your heart

Take no trash from anyone else
You've got the right to be yourself
Fulfil your need, it ain't no crime
Cos it's your life and it's your time

When you've got love in your heart
Please don't lose it
When you've got time in your life
Please don't waste it
Cos it never ever comes round for you again
Never again

Dan Russell

ENTWINED

Two stars a-shining
    in the blue beyond,
Two loving arms
    to embrace you,
Two stars entwined
    in one.

Two eyes look down
    from the blue beyond
Watching, comforting,
Trying to say, 'Grieve
    not for us.'
For we are entwined
    in one.

For God came and took
Up, up in the blue beyond,
One star alone to shine.
Then came in His wisdom
He came once again
Two loving hearts
    too entwined.

Jean Gill

ANXIOUS HEART

Anxious heart,
    so alone,
        fluttered like a bird.
            till one day,
                you came my way,
bringing gladness to my heart.
        such great joy and warm love,
                you brought along.
and loneliness was no more.
        and the anxious heart,
                had found a home,
within your heart once more.

Iris Davey

COMPUTER

Meanwhile: hand-grabber
Decimates my looks;
No silky substance here
But silicone lips -

To kiss the plastic magus,
Electric blue wet kisses wet,
A fangle for old aged litmus;

Time is the crept half-starveling,
Porter of wire, model pupil,
Visage of intent!

Eye me, eye me, eye me
Small to the point
Of a fractal equation,
Hum all night,
Act human in your
Bank clerk stifleness.

I place on you a pair of glasses,
Black-rimmed;
You squint at my chart,
I think I turn you off.

Graeme Vine

THE JEWELS IN HIS CROWN

He bared his all, to flash at The Queen,
But the Lady was not for shocking.
She'd seen all before, having borne three sons.
To unveil a statue, her reason to come
To Newcastle, a task that had to be done.
So what was the point of it all?
He ran naked alongside her limousine,
And the Lady appeared amused.
The police swooped down, with a heavy arm
And soon restored an aura of calm,
The Queen moved on with regal charm,
Was it worth the trouble and fuss?
It's not good manners to bare all for our Queen,
Though, the Lady was seen to be looking!
His torso was slim, with a tight little bum,
To shock HM was his reason to come,
Was it worth the hassle 'cos all he had done
Was to show Her his family jewels!

Pamela Carder

EAR TO THE GROUND

This is my volcano
This is my heartbeat
beating -
Beating my blood through
the brain-well

Mute messages
trembling from the core of the Earth
making their way to the surface girth

They decipher themselves in sweet syllables
for those who want to know

They split open the cracks and burst
the faults with lava-buds
for those who want to know the truth

This tremor moves like a heartbeat
beating -
Beating its message through to you
Lay yourself against the Earth and
you will feel it tremble too.

Candice-Leigh Johnstone

PLATELAYERS - MY FRIENDS

My friends walk the iron tracks
With danger always at their backs.
To keep me safe - and many more
In speeding trains that drone and roar
Over countless miles of twists and turns,
As diesel oil compressed, explodes and burns.

Yellow vested trusted men
I pass them time and time again.
I know their walk and lengthman paces
And most of all their upturned faces.
My friends who walk the cuts and banks
Wholeheartedly I give my thanks.

R L Harvey

NEVER WORK WITH CHILDREN AND ANIMALS!

(Thank you to Philip Gross and all my friends at Bath Spa University, for making poetry so much fun)

Do you have to so *that* now you're wrinkled and ancient? Old people snogging - how disgustingly gross!

My thoughts precisely, I think we've been patient, can we please get a move on now we're so close to the end of our journey - oh! Please put him down or I'll choke on this apple and make myself sick and you know you don't like it when I am poorly. Harness the horse Mother - make them be quick!

They're embracing in prayer, so that you, my dear off-spring, may be dancing with joy till you're old and frail.

They're not! They're snogging - it's gross and disgusting! I'm going to be sick Mother, pass me the pail.

Stop your ranting and raving your sister will copy.

But she's clinging like ivy. Thinks she's still young!

At heart, darling daughter, Nan's sixteen and soppy desperately clutching at memories that sprung from the years of their youth, long ago in *our* country before we were driven away from our home. For years their hearts have been heavy and empty but now it's their autumn, now *they're* free to roam. In the fields and the forests where no-one will find them. We'll build a log cabin for Nana and Pops, edged with gardenia and fragrant moist moss, we will call it *Atlast*, where our journey stops.

I don't know who's worse, the snogging old wrinklies or Mum gushing over with fairy tale stories when she knows we are going to live in a slum, a glorified hovel, a vagabond's den.

When you've all finished rowing, I have a suggestion, a compromise joyous and sweet for us all. As the snogging seems to upset your digestion, at market we'll sell both the kids from a stall. With the profit we'll purchase a house with a stable, a small granny annexe for Derby and Joan, with what's left over we'll offer a dowry and sell off your mother before she can moan!

Susan Seward

THE SHORT CUT

There was no other way to keep poverty at bay.
Like a worm hole in space it would shorten the race,
Maybe I could ignore the face.
Age was against me, but this was a new twist of the wrist.
I'd paid the fee for, 'Hell by Linda',
Whose words were as Cinder's.
The quick route I'd used
Was now by others abused.
All nations met in her Union Jack bikini
Passports ready at the place of entry.

Vann Scytere

VIRUS DIRECT

I was knocked out by a virus,
Who came from outer space,
Possibly masculine,
Because he caused my pulse to race.
He certainly had his way with me,
As my temperature did rise,
Even my delirium took me by surprise.
My head it took the brunt of it,
My face was waxen pale,
With ghoulish eyes this virus,
Sure took me for a ride.

The reason for this poem
Is to warn everyone
A *virus* is an *ism* and *isms* are not fun.

Hazel Sheppard

PLEASE EXCUSE ME

I don't feel well,
I've got the flu,
A million things to do,
I don't feel like doing a thing,
Except write this poem to you.

I've fed the cats, the rabbit, guinea pig and wild birds,
Hung out the washing,
And put in some more, for the next day.
Now, I cannot think of anything else to say,
The important jobs out of the way.
I have run out of words,
So I'll end my verse to you,
And hoping I'll be able to send you, another one or two
Next time.

Jane Milthorp

KNICKERS - I'VE WORN THEM ALL

'I'm moving into big knickers!' she said with delight,
Them G-string things are ever so tight
It's no wonder they call them thongs!
Stuck in yer crevice, ouch! Burrong!
Oh yes, big knickers for me!
Nice and roomy and so comfy.
Bloomers were me Grandma's choice
Slack elastic *mmmm*. Up she would hoist,
Mum favoured roll-ons, for firm control they were a must
Pushing the fat right up to her bust . . .
And me a ten in me bri-nylon briefs
Static electric sparking me cheeks.
Now Auntie Bell 'ud shout 'Give 'em hell!'
French knickers were her passion . . . *Oooh* the height of fashion.
It's big knickers for me now . . . they're my taste
With a good cotton gusset and up to me waist
Ahhhh . . .
So roomy and so comfy
And me old fella says . . . *sexy!*

Adele C W Lane

SATISFACTION

She went to his cremation
- with her she took an urn -
she decided to take home his ashes
- to get at him
she'd long had a yearn.

He never kept any of his promises,
not one in his marriage vow,
so with a smugness she took home his ashes
- she would get her own back
now.

She spoke to him, via his ashes,
with the thought
it was well overdue,
then she made straight for the toilet
and sprinkled them
all
down the loo.

He requested they be spread in some garden
- her intentions she kept very hush -
and with a smile of pure satisfaction
she gave them
a very good flush.

He always had treated her badly
- and cynically always had laughed -
now, long awaited, she told him,
she really wasn't
'So daft.'

Diana Mudd

TO SET FREE

'Who's let Tommy out of prison?'
Asked mother, busy serving supper,
'Not me,' my posh sister said, I always
Chew my food; I've never heard of an
Aristocrat being so rude; you never will
Giggled my elder brother, he pressures it
Into a chair - so there.

Eileen Barker

THE REAL ROMEO AND JULIETTE

'What light through yonder window breaks' -
                                    'I'm trying to have a look,'
'You're nothing but a peeping Tom, now sling yer blooming hook.'
'If I profane with my unworthiest hand,' says Romeo with a grin,
'If you try to touch me mate, I'll punch you on the chin.'

'Is love a tender thing,' he asks her, full of hope,
Standing in the garden there, he really looked a dope.
'Are you deaf as well as stupid? I just don't love you back,'
Says Juliette, 'Now clear off or I'll give you such a crack.'

'Then plainly know my heart, dear love, is set,'
'I know you love me really, you're playing hard to get.'
Says Juliette, 'This sweet talk is never going to work,'
'You may as well give up now, you really are a berk.'

'O speak again, bright angel,' he calls up to her bowers,
'I'm going to start sneezing soon, stood here amongst the flowers.'
She says, 'You try, I'll give you that, it really must be said,'
'But now you're getting on me nerves, so go and boil yer 'ead.'

'Shall I hear more, or shall I speak at this,' he asks his love.
He's trying to look up her dress, as she stands high above.
'When will you get the message mate, you've tried for half the night,'
'You'll be no further forward if you're still here when it's light.'

Says Romeo, *'Tis torture, not mercy heaven is here,'*
'Now come on love, that's enough, or I'm off for a beer.'
'I know just what you're after, you dirty little dog,'
Says Juliette, 'You've no chance, not even for a snog.'

'Can I go forward when my heart is here,' he said,
'Go to Hell, for all I care,' she says, 'I'm off to bed.'
He cried, *'Lady, by yonder blessed moon I vow,'*
'I've had enough, I'm on my way, you miserable cow.'

'*Romeo, where art though,*' calls Juliette from above,
Hanging from her balcony, 'Where art though, I want love,'
'Now isn't that just typical, men are all the same,'
'I bet he's cleared off down the Inn, or gone to watch the game.'

Marisa Greenaway

THE LOCH NESS MONSTER

To commemorate ye're special May Day
A micht as weel hae ma sae,
Tae tourists ye're a great attraction
But ye're drivin' me tae distraction!
Doon at the bottom o' the loch
Nessie ne'er gies me a thocht,
Staunin' up here fir maist o' the year
Just in case *she* should appear.
She's sae blinkin' discreet
She maun mak ye greet,
Tae her existence some hae their doots
An ithers dinna care twa hoots,
She's mair difficult tae see than *Her Highness*
Oor Nessie seems tae suffer fae shyness!
A dinna ken whie she disnae switch on
Noo she's become and international icon.

Margaret Meek

THE HOOVER

'Housework to be done,' she said, she was a lovely mover,
Suddenly she gave a shout, 'Something in the Hoover.'
'Have a look,' she called aloud, peering down the hose,
Nothing could be seen at all, jammed up I suppose.

Get some wire, it's out there, in the garden shed,
Still no luck, stuck there, I've hurt myself I said,
'Go to the shop, they may help, change your trousers dear,
Ask if they can clear the pipe, say it's stuck, I fear.'

In a rush then off I went, no time now to stop,
Hurry, hurry, on the road running to the shop.
'Can you help to clear this pipe? We have tried in vain,
A foreign body in the works, I have now a pain.'

The lady in the shop looked strained, 'To our man I've been,
He had a look, took off the top, nothing can be seen.'
'How very strange,' I cried aloud, 'I'll go home once more.'
Hoover lying there, all apart, on the kitchen floor.

Then I had another look and gave a joyful shout,
There it was, shining bright, object up the spout.
Oh, the feeling of relief was plain for all to see,
Sitting back, at ease once more, with a cup of tea.

Alister H Thomson

IF YOU CAN ...

If you can keep your hair
when other men are shaving theirs

If you can pay the bills on time
and not forget my Valentine

If you can paint and decorate
come home from work and never late

If you can cook and serve my meal
preparing it with loving zeal

If you can keep my kitchen clean
making it your daily routine

If you can wash your clothes and put them on the line
making sure you haven't forgotten mine

If you can mow the lawn and pull the weeds
lay a path and sow the seeds

If you can drive me to work and back
and soothe the tension in my neck

Then you will be a happy man
For I will marry you . . .
my *superman!*

Raymond Spiteri

MASSIVE MAMMORIES

I am going off to BUPA to get a boob job
Costing over four grand, which makes my hubby sob.
The operation will be painful but, surely a necessity
I will be half the woman I used to be.
No more reinforced underwear now it's satin and lace
No more talking to my cleavage now it's face-to-face.
As for designer accessories, I now hold the crown
With the most expensive perky pair of tits in town.

Jackie Manning

FUN TO BE HAD...

That's a nice jacket
It must have cost you a packet
Yes, it did

You drive really well I remarked
As he cleverly manoeuvred his car until it was parked
Yes, I do

Wow, you were really good I said
As I got out of his bed
Yes, I know

Well thanks again for a good time
I'd better go as it's twenty-to-nine

He was such a poser
In fact a complete loser

So why did you do it
Well he is pretty fit

That isn't the reason at all
Did he recognise you from school

Of course not - I'm only the cook
In my uniform, he would never give me a second look

So are you going to pack up and run
Oh no, I'm going to have a bit of fun

Hello Tom - pie and chips, or would you like stew
What - oh no it's you!

Gosh, your face is a sight
Did I give you a fright

Me a cook and you the head
What will people say - here have some extra bread!

Carol Moore

THE THINGS YOU GIRLS WILL DO FOR A LITTLE EXTRA CLEAVAGE!

(Heart bypass at 87 years old)

'Hi 'ya Gladys, it's Kim yer . . .'
Thought I'd send a little note,
I'm sat yer seeing you there
With them tubes stuffed down ya throat.
'Dreadlocks hanging out ya neck they're
Like the back of a stereo system,
Your hands all stabbed with little pricks,
Oy! Here's me knees doc, you musta missed 'em!'

It's not much fun Glad, I very well remember,
but better than you thought the day before,
Not an ideal way to spend a balmy late September,
But in your bank now you've *Septembers* many more!

Remember when as a kid you tried to ride a bike and failed,
Bruised, cut and sore with scabs and aches and pains . . .
Then suddenly your riding, *tazzing,* speeding-biker-sailed.
Well you've filled your heart with futures now, there's
lifeblood in your veins.

You and me now Glad, we've a bigger bond
That's ours and ours alone!
In the family you're the boss,
Me the jokey crude *fat-fart.*
We're folk of doubtful morals
That this family can't condone . . .

Allowing strangers in rubber gloves to be fondling our heart!

Kim Swales

A Funny Poem

I received a little letter today
I opened it to see what it would say
It said write me a poem that's funny
Something to make my day sunny

Now? I thought, that's a tall order
I really think that's pushing the borders
Is your sense of humour the same as mine
Or am I just wasting your and my time?

So I sat and pondered and drank cups of tea
But nothing really came to me
Except this little offering I achieved
And hope you like it, pretty please.

Irene Roberts

A DISPUTATION

Said the Cigarette to the Pint-pot,
As the evening wore on.
'Is it me or is it my face?
While you remain in fashion
I seem to be in disgrace.'
Then raising itself in a superior way
With an air that was quite entertaining,
The Pint-pot was heard
Very clearly to say,
'Your argument is quite unavailing,
While I am as sweet as a pot full of roses,
You are just smelly my dear.
There's nothing but wheezing
And coughing and sneezing,
Such noises unpleasant I fear.
We can claim for our own
Neither praise nor blame,
So, be honest, let's have no more pretences,
You're just as much to blame as me
For disengaging the senses.'

William Sherratt

MISNAKE

At Cannes
a man
named Stan
did grasp
an asp
then gasp;
I fear
death's near,
oh dear!

Paul Rand

LADS' ARMY . . . REVOLTING RHYME

If you upset the RSM,
You'd better watch your rectum,
For swift will come from him behind
Big boot when least expectum.

D Shiels

SIXTY

Yes, I know it's naughty,
being around for so long
after I'd proposed
to shoot myself at forty.
My capacity for being a dead 'un
is a moveable feast,
a bit like Armageddon.
But unless something happens
to screw up the score,
the longboat will leave Lindisfarne
on the tide of 30.4.2004,
And as the flames
sink out of sight,
you'll be able to say,
'Well at least the old bugger
set something alight.'

Geoff Fenwick

THE BARMAID'S FAREWELL

The mood in the Kittiwake Pub has of late
Been morose and obtuse, rather degenerate.
Strong men who you'd think of as unflappable
Are sighing and showing they're incapable
Of hiding their feelings and instead of darts
They're asking for napkins to staunch bleeding hearts.

'Take a grip, men! Stop sobbing your eyes out in here!
You'll only end up over-watering your beer,'
Says the manager, Dave, who is trying kiddology
To keep upper lips stiff with psychology.
'On Katie's departure I've been told on the phone
That the brewery's decided they'll send in a clone.'

On hearing this news a committee then sat
Comprising of Michael, Ian and Pat,
Commissioned to find a particular chain
Of some DNA structured to make Kate again.
And by diligent asking of regular dipsticks
They soon drew a list up of characteristics.

The committee's research, tabulated, collated,
Indicated conclusively, when evaluated.
That most of the customers, given their cue,
Expressed strong opinion in taking a view.
The report that was published concluded quite neatly
By listing ingredients to replicate Katie.

'Take Sophia Loren, take on bits of Madonna,
With Mother Teresa, and a touch of Jane Fonda.
Add a dash of Diana, two shots of Bette Lynch,
Pour a soupçon of Lumley, and then at a pinch
You'll find you've built up enough female attraction
To make a facsimile of our Katie Jackson.'

Patrick Brady

PSYCHIC VAMPIRE

My daylight is swallowed
By your fearsome existence
Your dread and terror reign
Filling this space with the Devil
I grasp for the helping hands
Where is the help I need?
When you appear to them
They cower in anticipation
Your evil soul floods over
And enters their remorseful souls
The abyss where you belong
Sucks them in, no help.
I hear my deadly screams inside
Inside as I try to escape
I claw at the passion you gave
try to destroy all traces
You infected me, you infect me
I love know you repulse
They tell me about you
Unloved, unwanted, used
I see you and the fear returns
Why do you suffocate me?
All my heart has escaped
And left you alone.

Kate Marsden

THESE PETITE THREE-LINERS

A haiku is a snack, a bite-size piece
Of sushi. Such exotic fare provokes
My appetite for five more, longer lines
To slake a bookworm's thirst for nourishment.

I know that small is beautiful and yet
No sooner have I started reading these
Petite three-liners than it's time to stop.
For sure, they are a clever shrink too far.

Allan Bula

SAD, BUT HILARIOUS

Mum and dad, sister and I,
Mum prevailed upon Dad,
Now spring was in the air
We should go away for the weekend
Unaccustomed Dad agreed with alacrity

Those times, long ago; Henry Ford
'Any colour, as long as you choose black'
Our Dad too old for new ventures;
Charabanc, train timetables digested,
Puzzlement resolved - we're off!

My sister and I, eager preferences outspoken
'The seaside, the seaside!'
Accoutrements bungled together -
We had a wonderful, memorable, too short time,
Excited, red-cheeked returning home.

Next morning, back to routine,
School holidays, sister and self laying about
Mum busy preparing breakfast
Dad was about, 'I'll go and let the hens out.'
Approaching the pen, such sad, creepy cackling sounds

Dad's unaccustomed weekend had upset his conformity!
Fastened in the pen, no food, no water!
Those poor hens!
'Silly damned hens! If two or three of them
Pushed together they'd have lifted the flap!'

J Lucas

UNTITLED

When with a pal you have fallen out,
You feel it was her fault no doubt,
Perhaps you are right but just the same,
Just take upon yourself the blame,
Better to say that you are wrong,
Then spoil a friendship,
Deep and strong,
The ???? to ??? you just become
Good friends again,
The loss of wealth is much,
The loss of health is more,
But the loss of your soul
Is such a loss,
That no one can restore.

Frances Maguire

A SLAVE OR WHAT?

Don't worry dear I'll cut the grass and wash the car for you,
I know you've had a busy week, while I've had nought to do,
The fairies came and washed the clothes, then stripped
and made the beds,
the Hoover did it by itself, and then found all the pegs,
To hang the washing on the line, but much to my surprise,
it went and did the ironing, after all of them were dried,
the breakfast dishes washed themselves, as did all the other places,
after the week's meals were all gone, and put them all away.

The car went for the weekly shop, and picked up the kids from school,
I just sat and waved them off, sitting on the kitchen stool,
The windows washed and dried themselves, the dusters flew around,
and the night fairies made each lunch box, so I could settle down,
And watch the television dear, to keep you company,
for as you know the butler did all the evening meals for me,
The polishing materialised right before my eyes, the mop came out
and washed the floor, another great surprise.

The baby made its own bottle, and then bathed the other two,
so as you see I've sat around not much for me to do,
A week of sitting on my butt, not worked as hard as you,
in fact a bit of exercise I'm sure will really do,
For the bathroom will clean up itself, then put the clean towels out,
whilst the upstairs maid will run around, collecting washing all about,
Then she will bring it downstairs, put it in the linen bin,
and I will sit and read a book, so you can snuggle in.

To your big chair, which may I add, made covers for it self,
after it finished washing down the glass topped kitchen shelf,
The rugs all rose and shook themselves, then laid down flat again,
the cutlery jumped from its drawer, that's how the table dear is laid,
So take it easy love I said walking to the kitchen door,
I've lots of time to do those jobs after all what is one more,
No answer came from the front room, not even a small snore,
all I heard was the lawnmower, as into life it then did roar.

Kathleen Townsley

I HAD A DREAM . . .

A baton of knowledge
From the dawn of time
Passed on down the line
Racing into the future
Significant
Insignificant
Judge for
Yourself.

Karen S E Mason

NEVER TOO OLD

See the old oak tree,
shaking its angry head,
soon the leaves will begin to scatter
leaving branches bare instead.

The doors will not stay closed,
and leaves blow around the hall,
and one poor lady out walking,
could not keep her hat on at all.

In a week such a change in the weather,
heating is turned on full blast,
there will be meetings again together,
for tea and a much needed repast.

We're having a Hallowe'en party,
witches, broomsticks as well,
hot dogs with onions, sausages on sticks
and entertainment that will be swell.

You're never too old to enjoy oneself
and parties we like very much,
Christmas especially will be good,
with crackers, turkey and good old plum pud.

Maureen Williams

LAUGH AND GROW FAT

A saying that we all know very well you bet
and laugh and the world laughs with you no fret
well sirs this may make you do just that
many years ago now when I was a young kid
a job was to be found for little me no fib
it was to be taken by my mum to a bank you see
my duties were to clean the brass sweep the dust
from the floors get the coal from a cellar just
make myself handy like the lady in charge I must
tell you this it may make you laugh it may not
I heard this lady say, 'He will soon learn the ropes,'
in my mind thought um that's to pull the coal
up from the cellar sounded good to little me
'I' soon learned the said ropes silly me.

We the family of mine lived in a cottage yes
two up two down had a small outhouse
had to go across a yard you see it was there the
gas stove was situated also a copper had to be
that was for wife 'May' do the weekly wash OK
the toilet was also out there a part to play
in the lives of our family that I do thus say
our son Tony remarked 'it was the only home he
knew of where you could sit on the lav' agree
go to the said lav number one or number two
and you could stir the soup that's so very true.

T Sexton

ABSENCES
(Why did you leave? Why did you have to go, before we'd had a chance to have a word with you?)

Eric, if you were here today, here in this room,
I would apologise, and beg your pardon for my blithe
Assumption that you'd always be around.
All through our boyhood years, you were around,
Touch judge and scorer, the eternal secretary.
I'd ask about the unspoken, the unspeakable,
And query how things were, before you went.
Also apologise, with all my heart, for thoughtlessly
Parading so much happiness before you left,
For being able to recall only the years of laughter.

Nancy, if you were here today, here in this room,
I would apologise for our unseemly optimism
Before you left, before you went away
Into the heedless night. I'd beg your pardon
For misconstruing the nature of 'new lease of life'.
I'd conjure reminiscences of Tiree
And talk about the Lebanon, Jerusalem and Pentland
Walks, about our sadness that you did not come
To Spain, Egypt and the Orient. Lost opportunities,
For which we'll tend the pansies, rue and rosemary.

And Fergie, if you were here today, here in this room,
I would apologise for getting back too late,
From Nowheresville. I'd beg your pardon
For taking suffering as read, your remarkable
Resilience on trust. I'd thank you properly
For fifty years of friendship close to brotherhood -
Decades of kindness, worn like a second skin. I'd give
You two good reasons why we wanted to come home again.
We'd take her hand, and yours, in ours, and say, 'Goodbye,
Old friend. We'll tend the flame, until we meet again.'

Norman Bissett

LIFE

When I was young from 2 High Street Rookery
I saw my dad off on the Radway bus going to Radway to work.

But now I am getting older and now live in 4 Church Street
Rookery. Some time back Freda Beard told me to go to see
a young man, which I did not see; but later on I went to Ken Rans
who told me to see Dr Turner; who gave me lots of Gopten.

So now I am boiling potatoes and cauliflower and apples, and beef.

The other night I saw a helicopter flying through my curtains.
The dad of the boys car grey with bright lights said
'Can't you find anything to do at 12 o'clock' he said.
'I could find you something to do!' The helicopter made the sky
Quite a glow!

Marie Barker

DANNY

Were prairies cross, forests or
What's left of either?
Amid reactors, did you seal-steal
Or coast-flit, an egret, with tar
Coated wings?
The minefields, the mines.
Danny, what caused these scars?
Hypocrisy confronted?
The intimidation of clubs?
These marks are now your uniform,
The valiant vulnerable skin
Still there and we shall wash,
Let the emblems have health
Or the nearest possible thing.
More than surviving, war's other
Meaning must be your grin, your
Arms, the valuables, each resource
An ozone layer with little burning pricks.
Map pins for oil, for the disputes,
Territorial, for the dumping, the vapours.
What fire has the flag of your cacki put out
Scorched to the chest?
The flames, their imprint, that shield now
Is peeling gauze. It's a tattoo in reverse.
It's an entrance which hands, the face
Coming close can only hope to console so
The come ye back,
The sunlight, the shadow knows
That you did, that you made it.

Look Danny, you're here.

Stephen Mead

THE VIRTUOUS PEN

In a few days life whispered to me several times.
A few days later I have forgotten it all.

I therefore have nothing to write.
Stare at my expensive pen and cringe,
Loathe its formal precision and inelastic vocabulary
Its supreme indifference to the soul shuddering along its length,
Desperate in my ignoble attempt to

Trap the world
In two
Perfect lines.

Ailsa McDermid

THANK YOU MY SPIRIT CHILD

It's been a long while now
When your seed was planted - a divine gift
In my womb I carried you
My lifeline was your lifeline, we shared everything
Together we received nature's abundance
Our love, our feelings, our thoughts, our beings
All, in - harmony

Your first touch, caressing and reassuring
As if to say, 'Hi there, I know you know who I am
I am your Spirit Child and I know who you are my co-creator'
I, co-creator? - I marvelled!

It's been a long while now
When you made your debut one fine morning
You arrive strong and vibrant
Your first respire, your initiation in to this early-plane
Witnessed by the highest order, seen and unseen

It's been a long while now
When you cried, my spirit awakened
I held you close to my heart when you suckled
Our heartbeats synchronised
Without a word we understood each other

It's been a long while now
Your brown eyes beholding inner peace and love
Your smile, a tonic to the soul
Your delicate hands, healing received
Your first steps - tiny steps, giant leap to greatness
Your quest for knowledge, your desire for freedom unabated

It's been a long while now
A beautiful, unique child you have been
Your mission, a choice for you to make
Walking your path in life

It's been a long while now
The web of life's great expectations
Marked trials and challenges of co-existence
Yet, no judgement but gratitude
As we were bound together in love and in strength
Our lives flowing in abundance and more
Every moment precious
Every moment treasured
Every moment sacred

It's been a long while now
You knew me before the day of the day
You chose me to be your eternal mother
You honoured my being
Elevated me above the ordinary
Thank you my Spiritual Child.

Meg Aku Sika Millar

ORGANISED

I'd like to be more thingy,
Having filing cabinets and such.
I'd file away my papers,
It wouldn't cost me very much.

Why is it when I visit
My friends for cups of tea,
Their homes are so whatsit tidy.
What's the matter with me?

I couldn't manage a whassname
You know, in a place that's full of beer.
And if I remember to put the bin out,
The dustman gives a cheer.

Why is it when it's raining,
My wet feet begin to smell?
I passed a neighbour the other day.
He sniffed and said, 'Whatsit hell!'

I wish I had a visit
From Carol Smiley or Lawrence L B
They'd change my home into a palace,
So I'd be more whatsit, then, you see.

Until then I'll have to manage
Do things as best I can.
I wish I was more thingy
But, then, I'm just a man.

Jerome Kiel

PEACE

Don't try too hard to find her
For you will look in vain.
She doesn't want to listen
Her blind eye shows disdain.
She's vanished in an instant,
She's dealt her cards with care.
You go on searching, pleading
You find she isn't there.

Faith and hope, these two remain
When peace has turned away.
Leaving you with sorrow
And a broken heart each day.
When you least expect it,
The blue shines through once more.
Peace at last returning
Through that open door.

Joan Kingscott

WASHDAY BLUES

We're two of a kind, my washing machine and I,
holed up for years under the work surface, sitting
in the corner looking blank. We appear stable, yet
have faulty wiring, a screw loose and are breaking down.
We are regularly supplied with tablets, and swallow bottles
full of softening lotion in order to function.
No one can see what's going on inside while we buzz, steam
and bubble up, but everything in there is creased and faded,
coming apart at the seams. We heave ourselves into action, spinning,
shaking and banging about. Will we explode or burn out?
Just ignore us and we'll get on with it. We're starting to wander
around the room out of control. We'll have to call a specialist in
to put things right, because the longer we leave it the worse it will get.
What is more, we can't open the door.

S Greenhalgh

STEAM IRON . . . SSSSSS

Press here . . . and
Flattened I'll hiss with
Contentment.
My ear close to the
Surface . . . listening
To the scorching secrets
Of the perfumed blouse.
Viewing the torn, tormented
Tassel, tousled there.
Digesting the crumpled memory.

Aleene Hatchard

ACCEPTANCE

I am not some giant
I am not a hero
I am nothing special

I am but an insect in the
garden of life
scurrying to avoid
the aimless, blameless fall
of the gardener's boot.

M J Hawkins

To Lorna

Here's to a grand and gracious gal,
Who in her banker's role, and attire
Has been a noble steadfast pal,
As she pulled us out of financial fire.

Thanks for the closing of an eye,
And all your actions, good and kind;
As the trying years are passing by,
You are leaving a splendid trail behind.

You are a tribute to your profession
And when the ultimate day appears,
Your wise, and sensitive discretion
Will lift you into the highest spheres.

So, thanks again, to a noble banker;
To a friend, in strife, and in need,
Who has been a fine and considerate anchor -
You are a great lady, in word and in deed!

Ernest Staeps

GOOD SHOT

Cara Line-Shot never passed
the 11 plus she couldn't do maths
she preferred to take baths.
Never made a fuss though when
placed below the rest having failed
that test. In a class of her
own, often on the phone. In
a bikini by the sea with a
school grade of D. But eventually
Cara beat the rest with
outstanding figure, face and chest.
Rose in teeth, clothes very brief
a very good wage, picture on a
page; very well done. Sitting in
the sun having lots of fun.

Vann Scytere

A POEM TELLS A STORY

Pushing children on a swing
Watched by mums - saw them cling
When one declared there to me -
Those women say - quite secretly
'He loves kids' one child said
Down the garden path was led -
To the old barn and shed
Held my hand as she fled.

These opened doors of Old Barn
To my eyes, amid the corn,
Five young white kids here adorn
The straw filled barn, just born
There you see, five young kids
The woman said, our Mum, you loved!
Loving kids - so there you are -
As we fed them, child like star.

In my eyes - lovely that site
Five white kid, children's delight,
Both such pleasure to observe
As with them both, I served!

G Wilyman

A Ruby Rare

For forty years you've worn my ring
And never had I wished it were not mine,
For when I placed it on your hand
I knew it would remain
Until the end of time!

You bore my children without regret
And loved them both with tender care,
You tended them when they were ill
And rarely had much time to spare.

Throughout the years my love has grown
Though there were times of great despair,
We battled on and saw them through
With something that is rich and rare!

Your presence seems to light each day,
Although at times be ill at ease,
Troubled by some inner thoughts
But you are not too hard to please.

You are as precious as a ruby rare
And nowhere shall I find
A diamond such as thee,
For if I walk the many cities of this world
No sweeter being on this earth
Shall my eyes ever see!

I dread the day when we must part
For in this I have no hand,
But until then my dearest Joan
I pray you'll wear my gold band.

Derek J Morgan

GLOSSOP'S HEROES

Poised on a pedestal in the damp town square
stands the winged angel of Victory
soaring above the town.
Arms raised in triumph;
A victorious laurel wreath held high -
A symbol of honour - for who?

Is it for those etched names on the plaque below?
In neatly spaced alphabetical lettered rows.
Their only claim to the world - remember -
Lest it happen again.

The Great War's triumphant marching
led them to a foreshortened span.
Their blood, spent on a field of quagmire, in a foreign land.
The blood, red, like the poppies that grew in their stead.

Out of the Versailles un-settlement
once more, came the spectre of war -
A new generation takes up arms;
While serried ranks of white marbled
Remembrance, advance across the land.

Now we watch them on the telly -
those who survived it all;
Standing silent, proud and upright
for those who never returned.
As they march off with blazoned medals
the camaraderie is remembered once more.

In every town and village
On the 11th month, the 11th day,
The 11th hour, the Last Post is played.

Pam Cole

STARLIGHT EXPRESS

Shining stars. Shining in the dark
On a clear cloudless night
A falling comet shining meteorite
Light up the dark heavenly sky

Yesterdays star's on the stage
In the ocean space of, the ocean of time
Higher than the cathedrals,
Higher than the perimeter of the circles in the sky
The star fell from the heavenly sky
To illuminate with fire the heavily black sky
Yesterday's glory! yesterdays fame
Burning like a bright star
To illuminate the dark arena. Of the Eternal Stage

The stag beatles, with their antlers
Sing deep in the cavern, classic rock and roll
While the audience scream, for more and more!
Sell by date? Eternal? Time may hazard a guess?
Sir John Lennon, hang around the airport
But he never buys a ticket
Sir John, Sir Paul, Sir George, Ringo strike hard on the symbols,
Rolling Stones made from solid 24 carat gold
Today is the continuation of the glory of yesterdays events

A Royal drama, a Royal fairy tale
The Royal actors, actresses,
Clamour to be! The main event on the world-wide stage
Lady Di was a star! Shining bright on the stage
Eclipsing the glory of the other supporting stars
Imagine 'if' the Royal stars would have had to
Audition to play the parts?
How many others would be hopefuls?
Would have to queue, for days to get in on the act?

On with the show! Hearsay? Echo the whisper from yesterday
Willies and Garret. Joint winners. Writing a celebrity
                                    contract with Fame
Robby. Will entertain you, with Kyle the gorgeous dame.
He got his paws, on the dame, without being slapped on the face!
Right on the front page. To illuminate the classic pop fairy tales.

Hooray for Hollywood
Dumbledore the flight of the Bumblebee
On the Hogwart train, the Magical Express
Hollywood icons of religious reverence
In the valley of the dolls, in the twilight of fame
The living holograms wait near the back door, of the glittering stage.

Freddie Mercury, the temperature soar, way up high
One hundred degrees above super fahrenheit
Bohemian Rhapsody. Just a poor boy, in the tattoo parlour
With red letters having normal tattoed on his chest
Oh mama mia mama mia, mama miasma culpa Mae culpa Mae culpa
Beelzebub orchestrate the rhapsody.
As machine guns ejaculate the quivers of the staccato drum roll from
                        1   hell
Another one bites on the dust, and another one down receiving the
                                    sacrament of death
Hell's own angels scream encore, encore, encore. The audience scream
                                    more, more, more
Hard rock hard core hard rock hard core. From the core of your soul.

On with the eternal play. On with the show
Or the audience will get stoned and bored
The divine right of Kings and Queens. The fables of legends
Who are the script writers? Are they in Heaven? Or reside in Hell?
As spaceship, starship sails in the ocean tide of time.
On the edge of the solar wind, howls the thunder of the immortal
                                    audience.
The carpenter write, the box office is closed.
Tomorrow a new show shall commence! So get in the queue, to buy
                                    a ticket.

T Lawrence

LIVE IN PEACE

Give back their childhood
Where is there youth gone by,
What can be done in a world
Full of trouble, landmines, wars?

Tearing people's lives apart,
Tears on a child's face crying
Reaching out a hand to be fed
Hunger, sickness, sadness shown
Everywhere. Across the green and
Desert lands.
Remember war can start easy,
I say put down the weapons,
Guns and bombs,
I pray one day everyone will
Live in peace,
People's homes, farmed wheat crops
On plough to feed food,
Give them teaching,
See the best in the poor
Help wanted campaign through
Aeroplanes, boats and people
Life is chosen in everyone,
Show you care,
Save the children,
You can and I can help by
Stopping war and give more help
For a better tomorrow.

Antoinette Christine Cox

Morning

A few drowsy sunbeams
Open sleepy eyes
And scare away the darkness
As morning fills the skies
The trees begin to whisper
The birds begin to sing
And God's shining glory
Is revealed in everything.

Mary Cathleen Brown

BLACK DOG

Black Dog is back, lurking in the bushes,
Poised, near motionless by the rusty gate.
With meaningful sniffs he reconnoitres his territory,
Then silently slips onto the grey lawn at dawn.
He was there all night, waiting
to warn me of the day ahead.
I thought I spotted him, and you did not,
or so you claim - but then perhaps it's just for me
that he patrols relentlessly
with awesome predictability,
before the sombre sun rises to erase a shifting night.

Black Dog is here, stolidly entrenched,
hogging the ambered fireplace, blocking off the heat,
staring with contempt and cool discard.
Here mood is moodiness, silence seeps between the boards
and buffered panic pads my cell-like walls.
No rhyme or reason to cohere these moods,
just spirals of depression that corkscrew unchecked.
Brittle dog days tumble on and on,
Preservation goads my blunted mind.
No stock in trade of sensible ripostes to hand,
Just roller coaster thoughts - more downs than ups, alas.
One curtain call and the balcony will beckon,
no counsel to ward off destructive thoughts.
A walk in the park would do, but could I lose him there?

Black Dog has gone, his tail between his legs.
The Beast was bored, another plaything called.
A ragged toy to keep him busy was all it took
to lend me breathing space again - So, can it last?

Winston was right - No one can flee the Hound of Fate,
incestuously cloned, so deep within
that only dog eats dog can end the chase.

René James Hérail

GOODBYE MY SON

We are saying goodbye to our son,
Travelling from our small Irish town,
Past the little local schools,
The college he has left.

I came here as an eager bride
To where my husband was born,
Planted my roots down into his soil
Twenty years ago.

I tried hard with all the neighbours,
Their battles are still a puzzle to me.
Why can't they just believe in God -
Then live in harmony?

It's time for our son to go on board
He promises to write, phone and visit,
So I smile to make him feel better
But inside I'm dying.

The clouds are swallowing his plane
As he heads for the English way,
Lured by the city lights -
The promise of a better life.

I came here for the love of my man
But now I am losing my son,
To the country from whence I came
So long ago.

Doreen Hughes

MY FRIEND

When the swords of the cruellest battle
crash before my life
yours is the face reflected through
the blades that blind my eyes.

When life takes me by the heart
and rips my feelings out
you replace them with a single word
and cast away all doubt.

When the rain of hurt soak me thru
you cover me like a towel
dry my tears and plug my ears
so I cannot hear the howl.

When all is lost and depression sets deep
you appear just like magic
to make me laugh and cheer my soul
till life doesn't seem so tragic.

How can I thank such a friend
words could never be enough
but what you give is what you get
so I return it with my love.

Rachel Kate

CALL FROM THE SKY

Lord, you are worthy for praise in our words and reflections.
I feel your palm as prostrate fair from the sky.
Sip of love you give us. Sip of life you present us.
Seeking you in our reflections. Seeking you in our works.
If some day I feel you I will save from the world.
I am feeling you with my heart.
I am feeling you with my soul.
I want droplet of power to save from the world.
I am feeling you with my soul.
I want droplet of power to save from the world.
You are in my reflections, you are in my feelings.
The sky is my expanse, the earth is boundless hell.
I will find you in my paradise in our boundless soul.
The life given from you is life closed in my heat and
If some day I feel you I will save from the death.

Lozina Taylor

HAUNTS OF A PAST

There was so much to attend to,
Being a wife through the war,
Her fears for her family
cloud her smiles she once wore.

Her rations wee sparse,
days of laugher were few,
Dreams of holding her husband
never again did come true.

She stayed strong for her children,
since her best friend had passed,
And at nights she'd lay crying
wondering how long it would last.

The sights of the carnage,
the wrecked buildings and dead,
The explosions and screams,
cobbled streets flowing with blood red.

Sixty years have since passed
and with that hellish time over,
She remembers Dame Vera
singing the white cliffs of Dover.

She prayed for her children
as she wished them all well,
That they would never again see
another war-torn hell.

But with a modern day threat,
her children still worry,
That they may relive
their dear mother's stories.

For this terror between nations,
Fuelled by the likes of Saddam Hussein,
The cinders of hell
are starting to rekindle again.

Michael McLellan

FORGIVE ME IF I CRY

It's been five years since I said goodbye
I am sorry I did not mean to make you cry
Had no control of the things that I hid
Broke your world when you was my kid.

Tried so many times to call you on the phone
Your Nan said you were never home
Remember I told you never to lie
I think she may have lied.

Wonder what you look like?
Bet you've grown so much
Do you still have the gerbil?
Do you still have the rabbit hutch?
And I hope you are doing well at school
Please do not be a fool
And break the rules.

Remember to listen and to do what you are told
Hope to meet you before I get too old
Hope your brother looks after you
Just the way I wanted to.

Son I hope you know how much I love you so
And I think of you every day
Especially on the second of May
I think, silently I pray
That you think of me and love me too
I had plans for me and you.

It has been five years since I said goodbye
Forgive me if I cry . . .

Stephen A Owen

OUT THERE

What waits for us beyond the horizon,
The far horizon
If we travelled out with the atmosphere
Drifting towards the stars
Around galaxies
Avoiding those foreboding black holes in space.

What waits for us beyond the dark infinity,
Where time and light are immeasurable,
Yet measured in years.
Mere men cannot fathom this vastness
We are but a speck in the immensity
Existing only a fraction in aeons.

What waits for us if we're not alone
Will we encounter life forms
An alien race
Somewhere in the great reaches of space
Other life must breathe
Humanoid, mechanical or energy unknown.

What waits for us after we've exhausted
The life blood from this planet earth
Does civilisation become extinct
Or live on
Venturing and crossing the cold silence
Are we mortal beings trying to be immortal.

What waits for us in the blackness
Creatures unimaginable
Planets living on noxious gases
Or cold frozen worlds
Perhaps we'll never learn what is
Out there.

George S Johnstone

THE DEAD MAN'S CHEST

I'm marooned here on my death bed
So I'll let the truth be told
About my icy heart of iron
In my chest of Flemish gold.

Spices from the Javan east
Need payment from the west
We set sail from the Netherlands
With a fat, gold-bellied chest.

Broken men have greedy dreams
Of women, wine and song
And we, the broken men on board
Connived to right our wrongs.

We picked the weevils from the grain:
Our allies and our foes
And mustered arms at sight of land
And fought to end our woes.

We took the ship, we drowned the crew
Whilst drunk on German wine
Then grew drunker still on fever dreams,
Suspicion, rum and brine.

We whittled down the numbers
Till it was only him and me
But now it's me, my kingdom's wealth,
My sickness and the sea.

Paul McGranaghan

IMMORTALITY

The blackbirds haunting melody
The curlews lonely cry
These things go on forever
But man just passes by

The moon that lights the prairie
The stars that show the way
These things go on forever
But man he cannot stay

The sun that wakes the flowers
The chattering of the stream
These things go on forever
But man can only dream

The clouds that roam the heavens
The rainbow in the sky
These things go on forever
But man is born to die

The wind that stirs the branches
The waves that wash the sands
These things go on forever
Untouched by human hands.

William Pegg

FROM LOVE BEADS TO SPACE SEEDS

The age of the flower
Free love equals new power
What is your sign?
Why that's opposite to mine!
Come let us sing a song
These times won't last long
Kennedy is dead
Killed with assassins lead
The war comes soon after
Bodies piled to the rafter
The death of every son
Hell no!
We won't go!
Dinosaurs of our age
Taking the role to centre stage
King dies on April 28th
Standing forlorn at heavens gates
His dream gone
Like a remnant of a protest song
The march becomes history
Swirling in times mystery
The swinging youth
Losing untold truth
What was it all for?
The protests the war
What have we gained?
Now the ground is blood-stained
With the dreams of our youth
Scattered flowers of truth.

Teresa Whaley

THE ASCENT OF MAN

We've scaled the highest mountains
And ventured into space
And plumbed the deepest oceans
This creed the human race,
We've built the finest structures
And reached toward the sky
And sought to answer questions
Like what and how and why?
We've tested our endurance
And laboured by degrees
And engineered discoveries
To eradicate disease,
We've journeyed far as modern man
Beguiled by our inventions
Yet the battlefields of Mother Earth
Are strewn with good intentions.

Michael Gardner

CASABLANCA

Casablanca in the rain
Neon lights shining in the dark
Pictures in puddles
Hide a story in the night

The puddles jump with the wind
Colours bright come into focus
A man walks past
He leaves in a moment soon gone

A cry is heard . . . what was that
The rain comes down, just the rain
People are laughing
Getting wet is part of Casablanca

Next time you go to Casablanca
Stand and look into the puddles
Your imagination turns to romance
Can you hear that plane landing?

I love to see the colours
Hear the sounds
Alas my view
Was only from the film

Casablanca.

Carole A Cleverdon

MIRROR IN THE HALL

Your echo holds a myriad of secrets,
Imprisoned by a chamfered bevel.
Closely guarded by skilfully chiselled oak.
So swollen with mysteries, absorbed through time.
Suspended by brass linkage you wait to gather and withhold.
Never will you talk and never will you lie.
The grand mirror in the hall.

You reveal to me my Gemini,
I then witness what others see.
A tarnished veneer may need a polish to shine a fictitious
contented semblance.
Time carves out the grooves contouring flesh once freshly
glowing with innocence.
Never will you talk and never will you lie.
The grand mirror in the hall.

No one can pass without a glance,
You show the here and now.
Your emporium must have such hidden depth,
for never will you overflow.
The clasp of a stare, enough time for thought,
a glimpse of folk fleeting by.
Reflection is eternal and is one's own minds opinion.
Never will you talk and never will you lie.
The grand mirror in the hall.

Mary Morley

ALL CHANGE

Those familiar paths I walk each day
Past ancient houses and spacious lawns,
With trees and shrubs - a gardener's joy,
And well loved Chapel not far away.

Further on a statue stands supreme
In a square of lawn so lustrous green;
It takes command of all who pass,
To set the seal on this tranquil scene.

And facing it, in different tone
Are playing fields, vast and wide,
Named The Close, where long ago
The game of rugby first became known.

Quite suddenly the scene has changed
And the air is filled with lively talk -
Laughter and chatter everywhere,
For young people need to take the stage.

From pathways up to now concealed,
A hundred voices can be heard,
And boys and girls in different groups
Their lively spirits now reveal.

Then all is quiet and strangely cool,
For everyone has found his niche,
But I will always enjoy the essence of youth
Provided by those from this famous school.

Joan Mathers

I'VE GOT MY HEAD STUCK IN THE RAILINGS

I've got my head stuck in the railings
I've been here since quarter to eight
Some bloke said he'd send the Fire Brigade
If he did, they're seven hours too late.

I'm stuck in the stocks like a side show
With everyone peering at me
You'd think I was Chi Chi the panda
They all throw me buns for tea.

The word spread around quickly
The looters were quick on the scene
My glasses and moustache had gone
By the time the police intervened.

I've had the BBC here to film me
And ITN popped along too
It made me very proud when before a big crowd
Terry Wogan gave me an interview.

All the bookies are making a small fortune
Of odds on how long I'll be here
As they should what am I bet
On how much blood they'll have to let
Six to one he's going to lose an ear.

My next of kin came at the double
My aunts, my granny and pa
My mum nudged my dad and said
'I always knew he would end up behind bars.'

D A Sheasby

JOYRIDE

Who gave you the right to take it
The property that was not yours?
Who gave you the right to steal it
And the heartache you were about to cause?

Who gave you the right to take it?
It was someone's pride and joy.
Who gave you the right to steal it
And the life you were about to destroy?

Who gave you the right to take it,
Did you do it just for fun?
Who gave you the right to steal it
And to cause the loss of one oh so young?

Who gave you the right to take it,
Did you not even care?
Who gave you the right to steal it?
You just weren't being fair.

Who gave you the right to take it?
It will remain on your conscience forever inside.
Who gave you the right to steel it,
For the sake of a senseless joyride!

S R Thompson

ASUNDER

My spider plant is trying to tell me something
To its main body is attached by a long stalk
A baby spider plant a little way away
      Dropping down low
            in the way they do.

It wants me to put its baby in a pot of soil
So that it can form roots,
And when it has done so I will take a sharp knife
      And separate it
            in the way it wants.

My children are putting down their own roots;
They are needing their own pots of soil.
I should cut the cord with scissors
      To set them free
            in the way they want.

I wish my midwife had used a sharper pair of scissors
To sever completely the umbilical cord;
Perhaps then I would have been free of my babies from birth
      And not now have been
            in the way.

Jean Medcalf

ISOLATION

Trapped isolation like a rat in a cage.
Nowhere to run, all alone and afraid.
I wish someone would find me and
Help me escape from this mad isolation.
Around and around I run never getting anywhere,
Never getting to the door of freedom
So trapped like a rat in a cage.
Help.

Judy Balchin

THE KITCHEN CLOCK

Oh kitchen clock, your familiar face
Has long adorned this room.
Plain, unremarkable, but nevertheless
A comforting presence to me.
By the end of each day, you would slow down,
Too weary to keep up with time,
Rather like myself, winding down before dusk.
Thus a bond was created between you and me,
Synchronised in our lethargy.

Suddenly, a remarkable transformation took place;
After years of going slow, you started gaining time,
On my return home, I found you had raced ahead,
Of Greenwich mean time,
Was this a mechanical aberration
Or were you undergoing a mid-life crisis?
Making up for lost time, seeking to regain
The ground you had lost.

Was this a signal to me?
Should I also accelerate my pace
And resolve to do more each day,
Rather than amble through life at a leisurely tempo,
Achieving nothing at all?
My question hangs in the air unanswered,
Your face remains inscrutable, you enigmatic clock,
As you simply reply, 'tick tock'.

A M Drever

ANGRY ELEMENTS?

Skies are never angry; seas do not fret and rage,
clouds are not menacing, hurricanes do not rampage.
Accursed rain stopped play, but although spellbound
it ignores the imprecation and saturates the cricket ground.
No treacherous and malign cloud made the microlite cough and die
when the black wraith could be clearly seen anvilling down the sky.

The parachute drop behind enemy lines that goes badly awry,
innocent planners rage while several hundred idiots die;
drinking and eating lunch from their awkward laps
while watching yellowing pipe smoke curl over misleading maps.
A way of denying it is ourselves who host this displaced rage
if the play is not properly acted out on our carelessly set stage.

For we are the conquerors; mankind rules; OK
so the freakish elements and other forces must obey!
Forecasts never lie; 'The winds will not be strong,'
but the weather, as ever, does not listen and gets it wrong.
Fishing boats capsize and founder in a cruel force nine gale,
and the lazy cows will not deliver milk to the milkmaid's pail.

Buildings abseil down a hillside, unfortunate victims
of a vicious hurricane; did the spiteful whirling winds
destroy them intentionally with malice driven gusts,
or that bridge slow-waltzing to disaster as its metal frame rusts?
If the engineers' wind tunnel had been properly deployed
the structure may not have been so wantonly destroyed.

Should the moon and high winds be in unnatural conjunction
Venice will flood, her economy thrown into severe disjunction.
But are not her sallow willow underpinnings in a dangerous state,
rotting and sadly out of joint, well past their sell-by-date?
Never mind the evidence, or the scientists' warning,
put it all down to that impending horror, global warming.

How burdensome it is to have live at the end of one's tether
bedevilled by such unsuitable and unstable weather.
Except for evening sunsets, rainbows, sparkling dewdrops
and early morning mist swirling over mountain overcrops
flaring like Roman candles; sights to ease the troubled mind.
Well let's face up to it; the weather can be very kind!

Norman Meadows